MURDERERS AND SERIAL KILLERS

STORIES OF VIOLENT CRIMINALS

by Kay Melchisedech Olson

Consultant:
David R. Englert, PhD
Society for Police
and Criminal Psychology

CAPSTONE PRESS
a capstone imprint

Velocity is published by Capstone Press,
151 Good Counsel Drive, P.O. Box 669, Mankato, Minnesota 56002.
www.capstonepress.com

Printed in the United States of America in Melrose Park, Minnesota.
092009
005620LKS10

*J
364.1523
Ol 8*

Books published by Capstone Press are manufactured with paper
containing at least 10 percent post-consumer waste.

Library of Congress Cataloging-in-Publication Data
Olson, Kay Melchisedech.
    Murderers and serial killers: stories of violent criminals / by Kay Melchisedech Olson.
    p. cm. — (Velocity. Bad guys)
    Includes bibliographical references and index.
    Summary: "Provides short biographies of some of history's most infamous serial killers
and other murderers, detailing their violent, criminal ways" — Provided by publisher.
    ISBN 978-1-4296-3422-9 (library binding)
    1. Serial murderers — Biography — Juvenile literature. 2. Serial murders — Case
studies — Juvenile literature. 3. Homicide — Case studies — Juvenile literature. I. Title.
HV6515.O58 2010
364.152'30922 — dc22   2009032780

Photo Credits
AP Images, cover (Charles Manson), 14, 15 (both), 16 (all), 17, 20, 28 (Berkowitz), 32, 33;
    Fred Jewell, 26
Corbis/Bettmann, 6, 10 (Whitman), 11 (top), 12, 18, 22, 29 (map); Orjan F. Ellingvag, 43
Fotolia/Konstantin Kostov, 37
Getty Images Inc./AFP/Eugene Garcia, 30; AFP/Rogers and Clark Co., 38; Des Plaines
    Police Department/Tim Boyle, 24; Pool/Bo Rader, 40; Pool/Elaine Thompson, 36;
    Time Life Pictures/Dick Swanson, 13 (bottom); Time Life Pictures/Francis
    Miller, 8, 9
iStockphoto/Gino Santa Maria, 27; Kenny Haner, 23; Sean Goebel, 39; Stan Rohrer,
    29 (car); Stefan Klein, 45
Map Resources, 21
Nathan Gassman, 31
Newscom/KRT/Wichita Eagle, 41; Zuma Photos, 35
Shutterstock/Andy Z., 34; Freddy Eliasson, 19 (blue rope); hans.slegers, 19 (crowbar);
    Harald Høiland Tjøstheim, 28 (burning building); Jack Dagley Photography, 4, 44;
    Jiri Vaclavek, cover (skeleton); JR Trice, 29 (bullets); Keith Bell, 42 (disk); Michael
    Zysman, 25; Mushakesa, 10–11 (bullet holes); Oculo, 42 (background); Ricardo
Garza,   11 (bottom); rook76, cover (prison bars); Stijn Boelens, 5; Tom
McNemar, 13 (top)
Wikipedia, public-domain image, 7, 19 (top)

Design Element Credits
Shutterstock/Hintau Aliaksei (photo frames and masking tape); Jiri Vaclavek
    (human skull, skeleton); Picsfive (pushpins); rook76 (prison cell)

TABLE OF CONTENTS

Murderers, serial killers, and criminal **psychopaths** — who are they? What makes them do the things they do? How can they be stopped? These are questions criminal investigators and **profilers** have been trying to answer for decades. These people study the way a crime is committed in order to understand the killer.

A modus operandi, or MO, is the method a killer uses. It refers to a killer's preference for victims and method of killing. Stabbing young blond women could be one killer's MO. Another might prefer drowning young men late at night.

psychopath

someone who has no conscience, or internal sense of right and wrong

profiler

someone who examines crime scene evidence to understand the type of person who committed the crime

Some killers also leave "signatures" to their crimes. A signature is something killers do to satisfy their emotional needs. It can provide clues to a murderer's motivation for killing. A signature might be strangulation with a scarf using a certain type of knot.

A killer's MO and signature provide investigators with clues. Putting these clues together helps them figure out what kind of person the killer is. It often helps law enforcement catch murderers sooner.

Police work hard to see that killers face justice. Very few have slipped through the fingers of law enforcement.

Brace yourself for details of some very disturbed and violent people. These killers and their cruel deeds will never be forgotten.

JACK THE RIPPER

Jack the Ripper is probably the best-known of all serial killers. He carried out his murder spree in London's Whitechapel district in 1888.

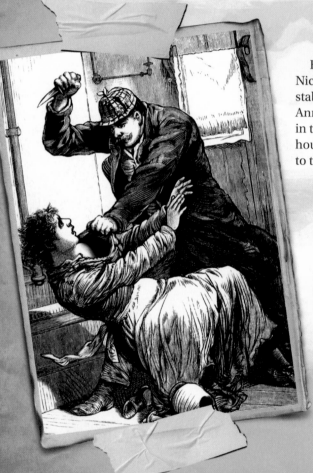

His first victim, Mary Ann Nichols, was discovered stabbed and slashed. Then Annie Chapman's body was found in the backyard of her lodging house. Her wounds were similar to those suffered by Nichols.

The police received notes from a person taking credit for the murders. He signed his letters "Jack the Ripper."

FACT:

The police received hundreds of Ripper letters. Many were fakes. The real Ripper did use a few identifying phrases, though. They included "Catch me if you can," "ha ha ha," and "what fools the police are."

Three more savage murders followed. The last was the most horrible. Mary Kelly was killed in her own bed. With privacy from the outside world, the Ripper brutally cut up her body. This was the last of the Ripper murders in Whitechapel.

locations in Whitechapel where Ripper victims were found

Jack the Ripper committed his crimes more than 100 years ago. But his actions were similar to more recent serial killers. He targeted women, stabbed his victims, and teased police. But unlike many recent serial killers, Jack the Ripper was never caught. Many suspects have been named. But to this day, his identity remains unknown.

ED GEIN

1906 – 1984

One strange little man living alone on a Wisconsin farm inspired some truly scary horror movies. Characters in *Psycho*, *The Texas Chain Saw Massacre*, and *Silence of the Lambs* were all based on Ed Gein.

Gein was born in 1906. He grew up on a farm near Plainfield, Wisconsin, with his parents and brother. By 1945, the rest of Gein's family had died, leaving him all alone in an old farmhouse.

FACT:

Gein's brother, Henry, died fighting a brush fire. When police found Henry's body, they noticed marks on the back of his head. At the time, these marks were dismissed. Some people now wonder if Henry was his brother's first murder victim.

Most Plainfield residents thought Gein was odd but generally harmless. In November 1957, a Plainfield woman disappeared while working at Worden's hardware store. A sales receipt led police to Gein's door.

Inside Gein's shed, police found the missing woman. Her body was hanging from the rafters. More horrors awaited them in the house.

Gein had also been stealing bodies from cemeteries. He peeled the skin off the bodies to create face masks. One face was that of another missing Plainfield woman. Gein admitted to murdering her as well.

Worden's hardware store

Gein's disturbing behavior went even further. He used human skulls as bowls. His refrigerator was filled with human organs. He even used skin to make lamp shades and chair covers.

Gein went to trial for his crimes. He was judged not guilty by reason of **insanity**. Gein spent the rest of his life in a mental hospital. He died in 1984.

FACT:

The body parts found in Ed Gein's house came from at least 15 different people.

insanity

in legal terms, being mentally ill to the point of not being able to tell the difference between right and wrong

CHARLES WHITMAN

1941 – 1966

Charles Whitman brought a day of horror to the citizens of Austin, Texas. In 1966, Whitman was a student at the University of Texas in Austin. On July 31, he killed his wife and mother. Whitman wanted to save them from the shame of what he was planning to do the next day.

Whitman's wedding day

FACT:

As a Marine, Whitman had earned a sharpshooter's badge. He was most accurate when shooting at moving targets.

The morning of August 1, Whitman put together some supplies. They included a sawed-off shotgun, a rifle, and a pistol. Then he headed to the 307-foot (94-meter) Texas Tower on the university's campus.

From the 28th floor, Whitman took aim at anyone and everyone below. No one within Whitman's sight was safe. Confusion and panic spread quickly. Radio and TV news reports warned Austin residents to stay away from the university.

Including his wife and mother, Whitman killed 14 people and wounded 31 more. About an hour and a half after the shootings began, Austin police shot and killed Whitman.

Texas Tower through Whitman's bullet hole

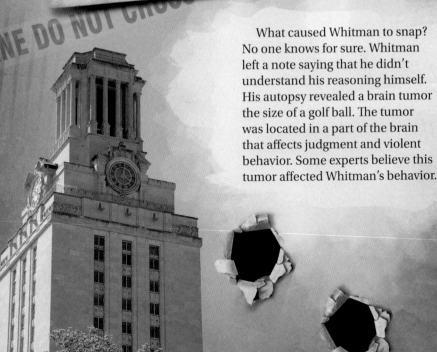

What caused Whitman to snap? No one knows for sure. Whitman left a note saying that he didn't understand his reasoning himself. His autopsy revealed a brain tumor the size of a golf ball. The tumor was located in a part of the brain that affects judgment and violent behavior. Some experts believe this tumor affected Whitman's behavior.

RICHARD SPECK

1941 – 1991

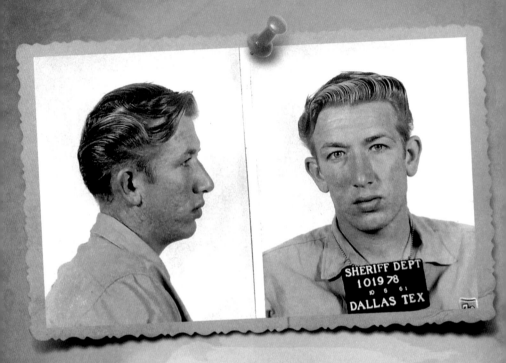

On the morning of July 14, 1966, a frightened woman perched on a window ledge outside of a Chicago townhouse. "They are all dead," she cried.

The woman, Corazon Amurao, had survived a night of terror at the hands of Richard Speck. Speck had broken into the townhouse. It was shared by eight student nurses. He bound them and stabbed or strangled them to death. Only Corazon Amurao had survived. While Speck was distracted, she had rolled under a bed and hid there. When he walked out of the house, Speck thought he had left no one alive.

Amurao gave police a description of the killer, including a specific tattoo on his arm. Soon, the entire city of Chicago was on the lookout for Speck. Speck cracked under the pressure and tried to kill himself. But an acquaintance found him still alive. Speck was taken to the county hospital. There, a doctor recognized the tattoo and called police.

Speck went on trial in 1967. The most exciting moment came when Amurao was asked to identify the killer. She walked up to the 6-foot tall Speck and pointed her finger at him. "This is the man," she said.

Corazon Amurao (left)

Speck was found guilty and sentenced to death. In 1972, the U.S. Supreme Court ruled that Illinois' laws about the death penalty were **unconstitutional**. Speck was resentenced to more than 400 years in prison. While serving his time, he died of a heart attack in 1991.

unconstitutional

going against the basic principles laid out in the U.S. Constitution

CHARLES MANSON

1934 –

Charles Manson (center)

Charles Manson chose a life of crime right from the start. He began stealing at a young age and spent many years in reform school. He also developed a habit of stealing cars. By the time he was 33, Manson had spent one-third of his life in prison. But in 1967, Manson was released. He headed to California.

In the summer of 1968, Manson set up a base camp at Spahn Ranch. It was a deserted movie set near Los Angeles. Spahn Ranch became home to a group of followers Manson called his "family." Manson controlled his followers with a combination of drugs and his own **charisma**.

charisma

a powerful personal appeal that attracts others

Manson told his followers the time had come for "Helter Skelter." He explained to them that a war between the races was about to happen. In the end, his "family" would rule the nation. Manson wanted to hurry it along. He thought murder would do that.

victim Wojciech Frykowski

victim Sharon Tate

Around midnight on August 9, 1969, Manson sent four "family" members to a house he had once visited. He told them to take knives and do "something witchy." Charles "Tex" Watson, Patricia Krenwinkel, Susan Atkins, and Linda Kasabian went to the house in Los Angeles. There they brutally murdered five people. One of the victims was actress Sharon Tate. She was eight months pregnant. The killers wrote the word "pig" in blood on the front door.

FACT:

One person survived the murder scene at the Tate residence. William Garretson was a caretaker living in a building behind the main house. He slept through the murders.

The next night, Manson sent out the same crew. But this time, Leslie Van Houten stood in for Kasabian. The group murdered Leno and Rosemary LaBianca in their home. The LaBiancas suffered more than 40 stab wounds. The crew left behind more writing in blood. Messages like "political piggy" and "death to pigs" covered the walls. The misspelled message "Healther Skelter" was written in blood on the refrigerator.

Manson victims

Steven Parent

Jay Sebring

Abigail Folger

The murders stunned and sickened people across the country. Police eventually cracked the case with the help of Kasabian, who never actually killed anyone. She agreed to cooperate with police. Manson, Atkins, Krenwinkel, and Van Houten went on trial in Los Angeles in 1970. Watson had been the leader in the killings. He was tried separately.

Throughout the trial, Manson acted strangely. He showed his complete control over his followers. When Manson carved an "X" on his forehead, the women did the same. When Manson shaved his head, his followers did too.

Susan Atkins (left), Patricia Krenwinkel (center), and Leslie Van Houten (right)

FACT:

Prosecutors never proved that Manson actually killed any of the victims. But because he ordered the others to commit the murders, he was found guilty.

Manson, Krenwinkel, Atkins, and Van Houten were all found guilty. Watson was also found guilty at his trial in 1971. All of them were sentenced to death. Their sentences were changed to life in prison in 1972. That year, the U.S. Supreme Court ruled that California's laws about the death penalty were unconstitutional. All requests for the criminals' **parole** have been denied.

parole

the early release of a prisoner

TED BUNDY

1946 – 1989

In 1974, young women in Washington, Oregon, and Utah began to vanish. Most of the victims were young college students. They were thin and had long brown hair. Many of the women had been last seen talking to a handsome man with a Volkswagen Beetle. Some witnesses remembered seeing a cast on his arm. Others said it was on his leg. A few people heard the man say his name was Ted. One woman, Carol DeRonch, managed to escape when the man tried to handcuff her.

Police were unable to find DeRonch's attacker. Then, in 1975, young women began vanishing in Colorado as well. Bodies were soon discovered on Taylor Mountain in Washington.

Taylor Mountain

One year later, a Utah highway patrolman stopped a man in a Volkswagen Beetle. Inside the car, the patrolman found handcuffs, rope, a crowbar, and a ski mask. He thought he might have a burglar on his hands. The man's driver's license identified him as Theodore Robert Bundy. He was taken to jail.

Police soon began making connections between Bundy and the murdered and missing women. Bundy was charged with the kidnapping of Carol DeRonch. He was found guilty. While serving a 15-year sentence in Utah, Bundy was sent to Colorado. There he was to stand trial for the murder of Caryn Campbell. Bundy decided to act as his own lawyer. He was allowed access to the courthouse library to do research for the trial.

Carol DeRonch on the witness stand

On June 7, 1977, Bundy jumped out a second-story library window at the Pitkin County Courthouse in Aspen, Colorado. He was captured and jailed eight days later.

Seven months later, Bundy slipped through a light fixture hole in the ceiling of his cell. By the time jailers noticed he was gone, Bundy had a 15-hour head start.

locations of Bundy's murders

WASHINGTON

OREGON

UTAH

COLORADO

FLORIDA

FACT:

As a child, Bundy often shoplifted small items. He stole things with a sense of excitement rather than guilt. Experts suggest this trait is common in psychopaths.

By January 1978, Bundy had made his way to Florida. There he attacked four women in Tallahassee. Two of the women died. One of the dead victims had the killer's bite marks in her skin. Less than a month later, Bundy killed a 12-year-old girl.

FACT:

Other than a bite mark on one of his victims, Bundy left almost nothing behind to tie him to his crimes. This lack of physical evidence led one prosecutor to call Bundy "the man with no fingerprints."

Bundy was arrested again on February 15, 1978. Florida police connected him to the local crimes.

Bundy was found guilty of three Florida murders in 1980. He was sentenced to death. The night before his execution, he admitted to 30 murders. Bundy's life ended in 1989, when he was executed in Florida's electric chair.

How Did Bundy Do It?

Ted Bundy's appearance was probably his best weapon. He looked so normal, so handsome, and so safe. He added to that non-threatening appearance by wearing a fake cast on his arm or leg. He would pretend to struggle with something he was taking out of his car. Then he'd ask the young woman passing by if she would mind helping him.

Once a victim was close to Bundy's car, he would smash her head in with a crowbar. He'd put the unconscious victim in his car and drive away.

JOHN WAYNE GACY

1942 – 1994

POLICE DEPT.
DES PLAINES, ILL.
78 - 462 12-21-78

Clowns are meant to entertain people, but many children are afraid of them. In the 1970s, young men around Chicago had a good reason to be afraid of one particular clown.

John Wayne Gacy was a building contractor. He was active in politics and hosted parties for his neighbors. He even appeared at charity events as Pogo the Clown. But no one knew what Gacy had buried under his house.

Gacy's first murders occurred in 1972. He would trick young men into coming to his home. Then Gacy would attack and kill them. A few victims managed to survive Gacy's abuse. Some of them reported the assaults. Their cases were not yet decided when Gacy was finally arrested for murder in 1978.

Gacy's final victim was Robert Piest. The police knew that Gacy was one of the last people to see Piest. When they discovered Gacy had a history of abusing young boys, they searched his house. There police found drugs, handcuffs, and items stolen from the missing boys. In a later search, they found something even worse.

Many people had noticed a foul odor in Gacy's house. He blamed it on sewer problems. But police discovered the truth. The odor was from 28 bodies rotting under Gacy's home. After this discovery, Gacy confessed to killing more than 30 people. Police pulled five more of Gacy's victims from nearby rivers.

police removing remains from Gacy's home

Gacy was found guilty on 21 counts of murder. He received the death penalty. Gacy was put to death in 1994.

During his time on death row, Gacy enjoyed painting. His favorite subject to paint was clowns.

Dumping Grounds

Why did Gacy start dumping the bodies of his victims in Illinois rivers? He explained simply that he had run out of space under his house. One victim's body was found preserved in the concrete of Gacy's backyard patio.

DAVID BERKOWITZ

1953 –

Between 1976 and 1977, David Berkowitz brought terror to New York City. Berkowitz chose victims at random and shot them late at night. Some victims were sitting in parked cars. Others were walking down the street. Still others were sitting on their front steps. There seemed to be no method to the killer's madness. No one felt safe.

At the beginning of his killing spree in 1976, Berkowitz was called the ".44 Caliber Killer." His weapon was a .44 caliber Bulldog pistol. But then he started sending notes to the police. He referred to himself as "the Son of Sam."

Berkowitz sent the police a number of letters that increased the fear in New York. In one letter he said, "I feel like an outsider. I am on a different wavelength than everybody else — programmed to kill."

On July 31, 1977, Berkowitz shot a man and a woman in a parked car. The man was almost entirely blinded by two shots to his face. Amazingly, he survived. His girlfriend died at the hospital.

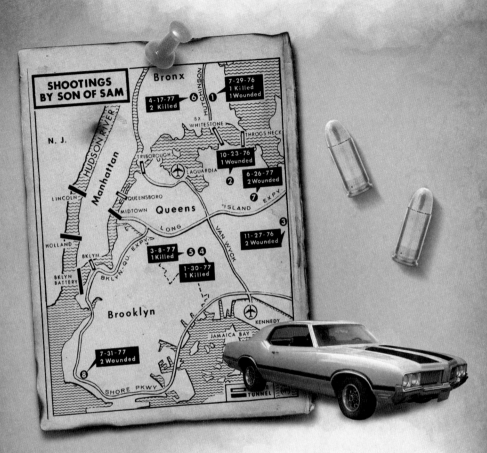

SHOOTINGS BY SON OF SAM

Bronx

7-29-76
1 Killed
1 Wounded

4-17-77
2 Killed

N. J.

BX WHITESTONE

THROGS NECK

10-23-76
1 Wounded

6-26-77
2 Wounded

Manhattan

LINCOLN

Queens

MIDTOWN

ISLAND EXPY

11-27-76
2 Wounded

3-8-77
1 Killed

1-30-77
1 Killed

HOLLAND

BKLYN

BKLYN BATTERY

Brooklyn

KENNEDY

JAMAICA BAY

7-31-77
2 Wounded

SHORE PKWY

TUNNEL

FACT:

In addition to being a murderer, Berkowitz was an arsonist. He kept a diary of 1,488 fires he set in and around New York City.

A woman walking her dog witnessed the shooting. She noticed that the killer's car had a parking ticket on the windshield. With the witness' description, police traced the ticket to Berkowitz's car. Berkowitz was arrested and **convicted** of killing six people. He was sentenced to 365 years in prison.

convicted

when someone is judged guilty of a crime

JEFFREY DAHMER

1960 – 1994

By age 10, Jeffrey Dahmer was playing with dead animals. He even saved some of the bodies in boxes in his room. Dahmer's strange behavior became more serious in 1978.

Dahmer had just graduated from high school in Bath, Ohio, and his parents had divorced. Both parents moved out of the family home. Dahmer was home alone and lonely. He picked up a hitchhiker named Steven Hicks and brought him home. After a few hours, the young man wanted to leave. But Dahmer didn't want to be alone. He grabbed a barbell and smashed Hicks' head. Then he strangled him. Hicks was Dahmer's first victim.

Eventually, Dahmer moved to Milwaukee, Wisconsin. He sometimes brought home men he had recently met. Many of these men were never seen again.

Most of Dahmer's crimes took place at the Oxford Apartments in Milwaukee. Between May and July of 1991, Dahmer killed almost one victim every week.

Dahmer tried bizarre experiments too. While his victims were still alive, he made holes in their heads and injected them with chemicals. Later he explained that he was trying to create zombies who would obey him.

Dahmer's 13th victim was a 14-year-old boy. He escaped from Dahmer's apartment. Neighbors saw the beaten boy and called police. The boy had been drugged and wasn't making sense. Dahmer soon arrived on the scene. He appeared calm and made up a lie to explain the situation. Police let Dahmer take the boy back to his apartment. There Dahmer strangled him.

On July 22, 1991, a man flagged down a Milwaukee police car. He had a handcuff attached to his wrist. The man told police officers that another man had tried to handcuff him. When the man led police back to Dahmer's apartment, they were shocked.

Dahmer's 13th victim,
Konerak Sinthasomphone

decompose

to rot or decay

There was a **decomposing** body in Dahmer's bedroom. His refrigerator contained several human heads. A large barrel of chemicals held various body parts. Dahmer was arrested. The details of his evil deeds quickly unfolded.

At his trial, Dahmer was sentenced to 957 years in prison. He served less than three years of his sentence. In July 1994, Dahmer was killed by a fellow prisoner.

Anne Schwartz reported on the Dahmer trial for the *Milwaukee Sentinel*. She later wrote a book about the case. Schwartz was surprised at how normal Dahmer looked and sounded at his trial. "I could see how so many were taken in by him," she said.

police removing remains from Dahmer's apartment

Guarding a Killer

Public hatred of Dahmer was very high during his trial. But according to the law, Dahmer was innocent until proven guilty. Special security measures were taken to keep Dahmer safe. Each day a bomb-sniffing dog searched the courtroom before anyone could enter. Spectators had to pass through a metal detector. Inside the courtroom, steel and bulletproof glass separated Dahmer from the rest of the courtroom.

GARY RIDGWAY

1949 –

In the early 1980s, almost 50 women in Seattle and Tacoma, Washington, went missing. Many were teenage runaways. These young women had no contact with their families. Because of this, few were reported missing. Soon their bodies started showing up in and around the Green River. The press called the killer the Green River killer.

Seattle, Washington

All of the victims were strangled. But their remains had some differences. Some bodies were clothed, but many were not. The killer had posed some of the bodies. Others he had simply dumped.

Some victims were found in the Green River. Others were found in nearby woods. Another dump site was a local airport. The Green River killer purposely changed his dumping habits to confuse investigators.

police removing remains from the Green River

Throughout the 20-year hunt for the Green River killer, police considered many suspects. Gary Leon Ridgway was one of them. In 1984, Ridgway took a polygraph, or lie detector, test. He denied having anything to do with the murders. The test said he was telling the truth.

But the Green River killer had left his **DNA** on four of his victims. In 2001, that DNA was identified as Gary Ridgway's.

DNA

material in cells that gives people their individual characteristics; DNA stands for deoxyribonucleic acid.

Police arrested Ridgway. He eventually accepted a **plea bargain**. The plea bargain saved him from facing the death penalty. In return, Ridgway admitted to 48 murders and helped investigators locate other victims. He is responsible for more murders than any other serial killer in U.S. history. Ridgway is currently serving life without parole at the Washington State Penitentiary.

Ridgway at his trial

plea bargain

an agreement that lets a defendant plead guilty and receive a lesser sentence in exchange for something

Ridgway's third wife, Judith, said that he had always treated her well. After their marriage in 1988, Ridgway did slow down his killing spree. He did not stop completely, however.

How Did He Pass?

How did Gary Ridgway pass a lie detector test when he committed the crimes? The best explanation is that he is a psychopath. A psychopath is a person who is self-centered and has no conscience. Even though he or she may know something is wrong, it doesn't feel wrong to him or her. When most people tell a lie, their heart rate goes up, and they may sweat. A lie detector test measures these physical changes. But when psychopaths lie, they don't feel like they're doing anything wrong. Their bodies don't respond any differently than if they were telling the truth.

TED KACZYNSKI

1942 –

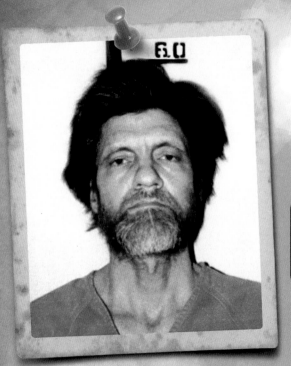

Ted Kaczynski was a childhood genius. By the age of 25, he had a PhD in mathematics. His professional future seemed promising.

FACT:

When he was 10, Kaczynski's IQ was measured at 167. The average score is 100. Albert Einstein's score was 160.

But in 1971, Kaczynski left his old life behind. He moved to a shack near Lincoln, Montana. Kaczynski rejected modern technology. His cabin had no electricity or running water. He believed everyone should live this way.

By 1978, Kaczynski had decided to get his point across with force. He began building bombs. Kaczynski targeted people and places where technology was thriving. Universities and airlines were his favorite targets. This led people to give him the nickname "Unabomber."

Kaczynski's intelligence made him a deadly killer who was hard to catch. During a period of 17 years, he made at least 16 bombs. Kaczynski's bombs injured 22 people and killed three.

Unabomber target, University of California, Berkeley

In 1995, Kaczynski sent a long essay to the *New York Times*. It stated his reasons for committing his crimes. Both the *New York Times* and the *Washington Post* printed the essay. Kaczynski's brother, David, read the essay. He thought the writing sounded familiar and tipped off authorities that Ted might be the bomber.

FACT:

The Unabomber case was the United States' most expensive hunt for a serial killer.

Kaczynski was arrested in 1996. He was convicted of murder. Kaczynski is currently serving a life sentence without the possibility of parole.

DENNIS RADER

The BTK strangler terrorized the people of Wichita, Kansas, for more than 30 years. Dennis Rader came up with his own nickname. It was short for his signature "bind-torture-kill" crimes. Rader especially enjoyed tying up his victims before killing them.

FACT:

"I wanted power. I guess that's what I was really looking for." — Dennis Rader

Rader's first victims were Joseph, Julie, Joey, and Josie Otero, four members of a Wichita family. Rader went on to kill at least six more people.

Only one person managed to escape Rader. Kevin Bright survived two gunshot wounds to the head. Rader killed Bright's 21-year-old sister, Kathryn.

Rader was careful enough not to get caught. But he was so disturbed, he wanted recognition for the horrible crimes he committed. Rader didn't think his murders received enough attention. He **anonymously** contacted the local media. "How many do I have to kill," he asked, "before I get my name in the paper or some national attention?"

anonymous

written, done, or given by a person whose name is not known or made public

Suddenly, in 1991, the BTK killings stopped. Investigators thought the killer might have died, moved, or been jailed for another crime.

But in 2004, BTK resurfaced. He sent letters to the police detailing his crimes. In one letter he asked, "If I send you a [computer] disk, will it be traceable?" He instructed the police to put an ad in the newspaper to answer his question. If the disk couldn't be traced, police were to publish the message "Rex, it will be OK." The police did just that. They were lying.

A few days later, the local TV station received a purple computer disk in the mail. The people at KAKE-TV turned it over to the police.

It wasn't long before police traced the disk to a computer at Christ Lutheran Church. Dennis Rader was the congregation's president. He used the computer often.

Rader was arrested, and he soon confessed to his crimes. Today Dennis Rader is serving a 175-year sentence.

Serial killers and other murderers think and act horribly. We may never understand why they do what they do. Their own words give us a small glimpse into their strange ways of thinking.

In 1996, Richard Speck was interviewed inside Illinois' Statesville Prison. He said, "If they only knew how much fun I was having, they'd turn me loose."

When questioned about his killing spree, Ted Bundy said, "What's one less person on the face of the earth anyway?"

Of his victims, David Berkowitz said, "I didn't want to hurt them. I only wanted to kill them."

In his confession, Jeffrey Dahmer stated, "It's hard for me to believe that a human being could have done what I've done, but I know that I did it."

Dennis Rader remarked of his murders, "I remember every detail from every crime. I remember every detail like most people do their favorite movie, and I play it over and over again inside my head."

The pain murderers cause their victims and the devastation they cause victims' families is impossible to measure. Luckily, none of these killers is in a position to hurt innocent people ever again.

GLOSSARY

anonymous (uh-NON-uh-muhss) — written, done, or given by a person whose name is not known or made public

autopsy (AW-top-see) — a detailed study of a dead body to determine the cause and manner of death

charisma (kuh-RIZ-muh) — a powerful personal appeal that attracts a great number of people

convicted (kuhn-VIKT-uhd) — when someone is judged guilty of a crime

decompose (dee-kuhm-POHZ) — to rot or decay

DNA (dee-en-AY) — material in cells that gives people their individual characteristics; DNA stands for deoxyribonucleic acid.

insanity (in-SAN-uh-tee) — being mentally ill to the point of not being able to tell the difference between right and wrong

parole (puh-ROLE) — the early release of a prisoner, usually for good behavior, on the condition that the person obeys the law

plea bargain (PLEE BAR-guhn) — an agreement that permits a defendant to plead guilty and receive a lesser sentence in exchange for something

profiler (PROH-file-uhr) — someone who examines crime scene evidence to gain an understanding of the type of person who likely committed it

psychopath (SYE-kuh-path) — someone who has no conscience, or internal sense of right and wrong

unconstitutional (uhn-kon-stuh-TOO-shuh-nuhl) — not in keeping with the basic principles or laws set forth in the constitution of the United States

READ MORE

Beres, D. B. *Killer at Large: Criminal Profilers and the Cases They Solve!* 24/7, Science Behind the Scenes. New York: Franklin Watts, 2007.

Newton, Michael. *Serial Killers.* Criminal Investigations. New York: Chelsea House, 2008.

Yancey, Diane. *Tracking Serial Killers.* Crime Scene Investigations. Farmington Hills, Mich.: Lucent Books, 2007.

INTERNET SITES

FactHound offers a safe, fun way to find Internet sites related to this book. All of the sites on FactHound have been researched by our staff.

Here's all you do:

Visit *www.facthound.com*

FactHound will fetch the best sites for you!

INDEX